D0054510

also by ntozake shange

theatre
three pieces
spell #7
a photograph: lovers in motion
boogie woogie landscapes

poetry
nappy edges
a daughter's geography
ridin' the moon in texas
the love space demands

fiction
Sassafrass, Cypress & Indigo
Betsey Brown
Liliane

by ntozake shange and Ifa Bayeza
Some Sing, Some Cry

for colored girls who have considered suicide/ when the rainbow is enuf

a choreopoem/

ntozake shange

scribner
new york   london   toronto   sydney

SCRIBNER

A Division of Simon & Schuster, Inc.

1230 Avenue of the Americas

New York, NY 10020

This Scribner trade paperback edition November 2010

SCRIBNER and design are registered trademarks of The Gale Group, Inc., used under license by Simon & Schuster, Inc., the publisher of this work.

For information about special discounts for bulk purchases, please contact Simon & Schuster Special Sales at 1-866-506-1949 or business@simonandschuster.com.

The Simon & Schuster Speakers Bureau can bring authors to your live event. For more information or to book an event contact the Simon & Schuster Speakers Bureau at 1-866-248-3049 or visit our website at www.simonspeakers.com.

Manufactured in the United States of America

30   29   28   27   26

Library of Congress Control Number: 8832633

ISBN: 978-0-684-84326-1

ISBN: 978-1-4516-2415-1 (ebook)

for the spirits of my grandma
viola benzena murray owens
and my great-aunt
effie owens josey
and always
my dearest mami & papi

for colored girls who
have considered suicide/
when the rainbow is enuf

Beginning, Middles and New Beginnings— A Mandala for Colored Girls

Musings and Meditations on the Occasion of the Second Publication

By Ntozake Shange

for colored girls began in the middle of itself. One early San Francisco evening when I could walk in circles through fog, I felt I was skipping through the mists, rinsing myself in damp clouds, licking the salty sweat at night. I started Cypress' diary: I am outside St. Louis and this is for colored girls who have moved to the ends of their own rainbows. Later Cypress became the second daughter in *Sassafrass, Cypress & Indigo.* My pieces seemed to fold in on each other and I fed them into each other. My girls in varied colors in all of my works, from Betsey Brown to Liliane, live in the journey of this work, were born in the journey of this work, *for colored girls.* From solo voice to theatre, from poetry to play, from random order to the rainbow, *for colored girls* has always encompassed them all.

The poems finding their way through me to the audience, for that story, let me go back to the beginning, one of many. In 1975, Paula Moss, a dancer with an MFA from Irvine, and I drove across country from San Francisco with *for colored girls* in its nascent form to perform at the alternative Newport Jazz Festival at Studio Rivbea in Lower Manhattan. We had no idea of the momentous theatrical journey we were beginning.

My sister Ifa Bayeza saw that performance and had a larger vision of *for colored girls* than I had ever imagined. A playwright, Ifa had been trying for years to convince me to allow others to speak my words, to let theatre artists do my work. As a committed solo spoken-word artist, I was suspect and resistant. I had never even considered having a director. I was a performance poet, not a theatre artist.

Immediately after the Rivbea I began to book new performances in New York. I stapled offset printed posters to telephone poles throughout the city. I came with my own things, and my own ideas. I didn't think I needed a director, but I consented to meeting a young recent graduate from the NYU theatre school, whom Ifa had pegged as compatible.

When I first met Oz Scott, I was dubious. At the height of 6'4" and with his long patrician nose, Oz had the immediate appearance of a man looking down on the world. A Charles de Gaulle from Mount Vernon. He proved, however, to be disarmingly warm and self-effacing, and while quiet to the point of concern in casual conversation, he was so animated in his enthusiasm for my words and about his vision for them, that he won me over.

What does a director do? I asked. I had scheduled a new performance at Old Reliable, a galley bar on Avenue D in the East Village. When I came to the first rehearsal I immediately saw Oz's influence. He had assembled a group of actors, five young women. The five added to Paula and myself became seven, the rainbow. Oz had made such a

2/

natural leap, physicalizing the image, giving the rainbow a human form. I was suddenly surrounded by a circle of women, sacred in construction. My solo voice began its journey to many voices. We bonded immediately and worked with an effortless excitement. While that ensemble would change slightly in the months ahead, the core ensemble remained as it was that first day: myself and Paula Moss, Aku Kadogo, Laurie Carlos, and Trazana Beverley. Later Janet League and Rise Collins completed the set of seven. My sister Ifa sat in occasionally as a second pair of eyes and ears. Oz and I immediately began experimenting, collaborating with the ensemble, matching individual pieces to personalities.

The poem "now i love somebody more than" went to the fiery Laurie Carlos with the husk of her voice and the sassy pop of her *p*'s in "my poppa thought he was Puerto Rican." "toussaint" went to the doe-eyed Janet League, discovering her hero and that first touch of love. Both of these poems are journey poems. In each a young girl runs away with dreams of discovery. One yearns to travel down the Mississippi, the other up up up the stairs to a project party. The poems introduce the girls to other kinds of people of color, other worlds. To adventure, and kindness, and cruelty. Cruelty that we usually think we face alone, but we don't. We discover that by sharing with each other we find strength to go on. The poems are the play's first hint of the global misogyny that we women face.

The ensemble was organic, fluid, and collaborative, all of us learning while doing. Through improvisation, we discovered and enhanced the beginning of the drama. We encountered the children's games Miss

Mary Mack, hopscotch, ring dances, common games which drew most girls of color into a public arena, exhibiting coordination, verbal pyrotechnics, and early sexuality. I watched grown women find the child in themselves, unabashedly shedding the structured worlds their parents had offered them for one of their own making, the secret life of girls.

From this cloistered circle, all fall down. A girl, a colored girl, journeys again into the wider world, the arbitrary and foreign. "no more love poems" #1 thru #4, "sorry," "pyramid," and "somebody almost walked off wid alla my stuff" allow the women to find humor in their various situations, knowing finally that they are not suffering all by themselves.

"somebody almost walked off wid alla my stuff" I wrote after overhearing the banter of women in Dianne McIntyre's dance class in Harlem. I had rushed out of rehearsal in lower New York to get to Dianne's audition for her new ensemble and for coveted scholarships. The chatter as we women dressed was about men, life, and stuff. During tryouts, a young dancer, Mickey Davidson, who later became my excellent friend, leaped so high with her jetés that Dianne had her do the floor exercise with the men, and she was still two feet higher, her head dangerously close to the ceiling. That power and grace flew into the words, so that the poem became not a lament but a fierce declaration of independence.

Throughout that spring and summer, I added and took away poems. Poems were still finding their place. "sechita" took a while. It was the only poem in the series outside contemporary time. Sechita is an Egyptian goddess of creativity and filth. Next to Beau Willie, she is the most misunderstood character in *for colored girls*. I created "sechita" in a class I was teaching at Sonoma State University in California. I had given my students an in-session assignment to look at a classmate and imagine who else she or he could be in any time or culture. To cross-check their effectiveness, I always do my exercises along with my classes. I chose a young woman who was so opalescent and lovely, her eyes were so sad, her cheeks so hard, she brought me to tears.

I immediately thought of fancy girls in New Orleans who had to find some kind of work after the Civil War and during Reconstruction. I knew there were carnivals and circuses even during slavery. I figured there would be even more during Reconstruction, with their bravura and freedom, opening the way for black senators and representatives despite the dangers associated with that time. While the audiences certainly were predominantly white and male, the circus was one world in which the lines of color swerved, giving African-American men presence and visibility. I knew that even if they were in the shadows or in the back of the audience, there would be black men watching her dance as well. The fancy girl dancing, her being is seen, independent, poor, and implacable.

I was unable to conjure anyone but Sechita, the goddess of filth, so appropriately blending beauty with gall in her performance. In working the poem in New York, it was easy to feel her environs. While the poem is set in the distant time of the post–Civil War, Sechita could just as easily have been a young woman working the strip bars on Second Avenue down the street from our rehearsal space or on the then seedy Forty-second Street, around the corner from the Broadway lights where the play would eventually run.

Still the poem was hard to place in both the sequence of verses and with the right actress. Sechita rotated many times until her voice settled in Rise Collins.

As I made my home in New York, new poems began to unpack. "sorry" was added so fast, we only had a day to memorize and block it before performing. "abortion cycle #1" I wrote in a rehearsal break. I made it short because I didn't want to go there, and that brevity became its strength.

Soon after we had worked in the improvisational girls' games as part of a new beginning, *for colored girls* got a new ending as well. The first inspiration for writing "a nite with beau willie brown" struck while I was still living in California. I was caught in a traffic jam; there were police cars everywhere. Finally I looked up and saw a man holding two children from his terrace. It was terrifying. Then, after coming to New York, I moved to a boardinghouse at 149th Street and Amsterdam in Harlem. There was no air. Then I started noticing these articles in the *New York Post,* the back pages. Three of them, I believe, one or two inches long. Stories of men dropping children from windows. The image from San Francisco kept haunting me. It was brutal outside, no breeze. Smells sat in the air. Through my window I could hear some man was screaming and beating his female companion, saying he should never have married her. Somehow the memories and beatings fell into each other and I began "a nite with beau willie brown." The fighting stopped/ the door banged shut. I called Ifa and read it/ just born. Pause. Silence her reaction. Then, "This is the best thing you've written. That's your climax."

When suddenly the Lady in Red utters "there waz no air," we are drawn into the tragedy of Crystal and Beau Willie and the children. Had I left Beau Willie as a mean and humorless fellow, his character would have been unbearable, but he sat up like John the Baptist with stubbly nuts, and he wanders like a hopeless derelict in his Washington Heights neighborhood. He wants to marry Crystal, that's all. Beau Willie is as desperate as Crystal. His only prizes are his children and his delusion that Crystal will marry him someday. It is such a complete story, compact in birth and death. The story spoke to the silent endurance of so many women. For me, in the writing of it, that woman, that one woman I heard screaming, was no longer silent. The poem as it shifts points of view gives Crystal back her life, her voice, but all she can do is whisper. At the last moment Beau Willie's saga becomes Crystal's realization: her life becoming her own at the moment of its lowest depth, giving voice to an experience so devastating, it would appear there is no return. Except through the laying on of hands, the sacred circle, the healing circle of the final poem.

When I took "beau willie" to rehearsal, Trazana Beverley wept the first time she read it. The second time she did it, she was so overwhelmed, possessed of the spirit, Oz had to end rehearsal and coax her back to us, the ensemble literally laying on their hands like church. There was a coming together, bodies moving into the circle again like the womb, and the healing light and power of spirit.

The first "theatre" for my new "theatre work" was actually the Henry Street Settlement House lecture hall, with seating for about a hundred. Such is the transformative power of drama, that, opening night, it became a divine space, supplicants flocking from everywhere. At dusk, the line was around the corner, the width of compact bodies pressed against the lobby doors, so thick, we had to fight to get in. "I'm in the show!" I had to shout.

Woodie King Jr., who had just produced Ifa's first play and who was employing Oz as stage manager for Ed Bullins's "The Taking of Miss Janie," came to see the show and decided to produce it. *for colored girls* was moving up in the world. From the bar on Avenue D we moved to the New Federal Theatre. Still the Lower East Side, but the street was Grand.

Three months later, at the invitation of Joe Papp, we were at the Public Theater and then made the quantum leap to the Booth Theater on Broadway. Truly, it was like ridin' a rainbow.

With the new venue came a dance studio with abundant light and a hardwood spring floor, space. But the work, just like a young creature, was still hungry. It needs something, Oz said. Having started in the middle, I found myself back at the beginning. Ifa asked me if I remembered a poem she'd heard me read when we lived together in Boston. That had been a year of poetry readings, snowed-in three-day salons, discovery. "It went 'sing a black girl's song' or something like that," Ifa said.

"somebody anybody sing a black girl's song" was written for my students at California State College at Long Beach Upward Bound. My students were predominantly black and brown with everything moving against them. One had so little sense of self, she turned in a poem by Nikki Giovanni as her own creation. I felt so close to these young women, I wrote that poem for them, my girls. I had a different gift for my fellas, who were pretty awkward. We learned Mexican folk dances and songs their families sang in the fields while chopping lettuce or digging for garlic. I wanted these both girls and boys to represent themselves with honor and joy.

I remembered the poem clearly, but we couldn't find it anywhere. We went through every notebook of writing I possessed. I began to wonder if I had perhaps dreamed it. We plundered notebooks, all the way back to my "phat moma's drumstick thighs" of my undergraduate poetry years at Barnard, when my verse was saucy and insouciant. I found a lot of memory-lane lines, but not that poem. Finally, out of desperation, we started calling my friends. I often sent poems as gifts, never thinking I would need them back. But Jessica Hagedorn didn't have it, Wopo Holup didn't have it, Paula Moss didn't have it. Finally my sister found it, and "sing a black girl's song" made its way back to me.

The next day we took the poem into rehearsal and I read it aloud, and heard the words myself for the first time in many years. Oz agreed that it was the new beginning we were looking for, the framing device, the anthem. Giving poems that had been on a journey from outside San Francisco and St. Louis and Chicago a clear direction, the journey now had a destination, a destiny.

It was all so serendipitous. The choreopoem took on an arc. Ifa's marvelous set with the classic central mandala in the shape of a flower, our first set design, gifted the work with a magical aura in which the actors found refuge as well as energy. The fluid dresses, designed by the late Judy Dearing, took on colors from the set design, imbuing each lady with a persona and each persona with a unique deific principle marking the journey of womanhood. The personal story of a woman became every woman, the solo voice becoming many. Each poem fell into its rightful place, a rainbow of colors, shapes, and timbres of voice, my solo instrument blossoming into a cosmic chamber ensemble.

Not everybody found solace in my work. There was quite a ruckus about the seven ladies in their simple colored dresses. I was truly dumbfounded that I was right then and there deemed the biggest threat to black men since cotton pickin', and not all women were in my corner either. The uproar about how I portrayed black men was insidious and venal. I was said to hate men, especially black men. Apparently my choreopoem hit several nerves. There were fisticuffs in Chicago, male students trying to shout me down at Howard University. My lawyer, David Franklin of Atlanta, considered getting me bodyguards. It felt dangerous.

Methinks the gentlemen didst protest too much. In San Francisco, I lived in a women-centered world, taught women's studies, belonged to women's cultural and political groups. The Third World Woman's Collective is primarily what I am speaking of. The show was literally *for colored girls,* which to me meant women-centered. Still nothing prepared me for the hateful response from African-American English-speaking males. *for colored girls* was meant for women of color. The poems were addressing situations that bridged our secret (unspoken) longing. *for colored girls* still is a women's trip, and the connection we can make through it, with each other and for each other, is to empower us all.

The reaction from black men to *for colored girls* was in a way very much like the white reaction to black power. The body traditionally used to power and authority interpreting, through their own fear, my work celebrating the self-determination and centrality of women as a hostile act. For men to walk out feeling that the work was about them spoke to their own patriarchal delusions more than to the actuality of the work itself. It was as if merely placing the story outside themselves was an attack. *for colored girls* was and is for colored girls.

Soon after I left the Broadway cast of *for colored girls,* Joe Papp enlisted me to direct a production of Richard Wesley's *The Mighty Gents,* a harrowing play that chronicles the lives of black men who, having bonded as a gang in their youth, grapple with the adult circumstances and tribulations that result from their respective chosen paths. Whether it was Joe's way of attempting to quell the notion that I was this literary castrator of black men or simply an experiment to see just what would happen when a black feminist takes the directorial reins of a volatile, testosterone-laden dramatic work, I don't know. My friend, Claude E. Sloan, who was working at the Public Theater at the time, reminds me that when he would occasionally sit in on rehearsals he could feel the air thick with the animosity that the male actors seemed to hold toward me.

In reality, there aren't that many negative images of black men in *for colored girls*. "toussaint" and "now i love somebody more than" present rather healthy images of black males. Certainly the follies and foibles of modern relationships and one-night stands as represented in the love poems are pretty gender free. Vulnerabilities and weaknesses of women in the abortion poem and "we all saw him at the same time" are apparent. True, "beau willie" is devastating, but despite his horrific actions, Beau Willie is a strangely empathetic character. I wrote the work to make an important, and yet unspoken, social comment. The poem articulated post-traumatic stress syndrome long before it was a national issue, and it was one of the first works of modern literature to give spousal abuse and its potentially dire consequences a harrowing voice and vision.

Per square inch, there are more negative images of black men in your average rap song or television cop show than in my choreopoem. It is disheartening to see how entrenched and celebrated the culture of misogyny has become. I dared to challenge and expose it three decades ago. The need to do so may be even greater today. While it was painful to be so maligned, I will pay that price as a poet to speak my truth.

Some men, like Stanley Crouch, will never like my work. Others now come to it with gentler eyes and less sensitive ears. They have grown. We all have. The preeminent poet Haki Madhubuti said it best. When I received the Gwendolyn Brooks Poetry Prize for Lifetime Achievement, Haki said to me simply, "We didn't know."

These are memories—enuf. What of the now? Over a hundred thousand copies have been sold. There are numerous productions every year. As I write, a movie and a new Broadway-bound production are in the works. My friends like to joke that not a day goes by when some young woman somewhere isn't doing a *for colored girls* monologue, making the voice her own, finding her own infinite beauty once again.

When Claude Sloan convinced me to sign up on MySpace, one of my first "friends" was a young twenty-one-year-old girl who had just returned to the states from a fifteen-month deployment in Iraq. She wrote to let me know that her dog-eared copy of *for colored girls* had helped get her through the harrowing and dangerous days of her tour of duty. She thanked me for helping her find and hold on to and cherish her own rainbow. Humbling.

People have done my choreopoem in period costume, with the ladies' colors representing different decades. There have been primal percussive productions with all women drummers; prison cell block concepts, the inmates vogueing and vamping for each other; beauty shop settings, the hairdressers and customers swapping stories; mature women radio personalities and high school troupes. In Rio, the Brazilian translation dropped the word *colored* from the text.

A white theatre company in Lexington, Kentucky, presented an all-white Appalachian version, doing a great job, basing the drama on class instead of race. In the first London production, the white director sat back and let the black women in the company tell him what needed to happen. There have been beautiful productions from Paris to Port-au-Prince.

I was recently invited to attend an opening-night production of *for colored girls* at the Oakland Black Repertory Theater. Upon our

13/

arrival, the cast exuberantly greeted us backstage before the show. I was surprised to see fifteen bright, shining faces, comprising so many shades of diverse ethnicities. There were two of each wearing the respective colors indicated in the work. And then I noticed one smiling face wearing a flowing costume that was awash in a beautiful rainbow pattern. I smiled, realizing once again in that moment how this entity I had given birth to was all grown up, out in the world on her own to be loved and understood and interpreted in more ways than I could have ever imagined for her. At the end of the performance as I was signing programs and books, one woman stepped up with tears in her eyes. Beside her stood her daughter and her granddaughter. She lifted up a shopping bag from which she extracted what seemed to be every literary work I had ever penned as well as an album, a videocassette, and a worn and tattered poster from the Broadway production of *for colored girls.* She said to me, simply, "Thank you for helping me to love my daughters fiercely and raise them right."

As of this writing the last scenes of Mr. Tyler Perry's adaptation of *for colored girls* are being filmed in New York. I had the pleasure and honor of meeting the cast and having lunch with some of the formidable women who will be bringing the work to life on the big screen—Whoopi Goldberg, Phylicia Rashad, Kerry Washington, Loretta Devine, Thandie Newton, Tessa Thompson, Kimberly Elise, Janet Jackson, Anika Noni Rose. Our conversation was surprisingly light and easy as we chatted mostly about favorite foods and our relationships to the piece itself. Some of the women had brought their paperback copies of *for colored girls* for all of us to sign. It was reminiscent of early graduations where we would bring our remembrance books for each other to write our good-byes and best wishes as we each prepared to take that next exciting step out into the unknown along our separate journeys. Ms. Thompson, the youngest of the cast of women, handed me a hardcover copy wrapped in a heavy clear plastic jacket. She laughingly explained how her father had borrowed the book from the public library when she was a little girl and had "forgotten" to ever return it. It warmed me to realize the wonderful possibilities that our literature fans in the sharing of words and stories across generations, continuously fueling new generations of readers to imagine and dream and strive. That *for colored girls* continues to resonate so profoundly almost forty years after I first set pen to paper is bittersweet for me. Though we have achieved many a milestone, the stories and struggles of our lives as women, and in particular, women of color, are still not granted the full address due. But, then, perhaps that is part of the fuel that moves me to continue writing.

As for me, despite the remarkable experience, exposure, and opportunity theatre has given me, my roots remain firmly grounded in the fertile hallowed ground of poetry, random poems dictating their own course. I have been blessed with abundant opportunities to continue adding my voice to the great human conversation through my writing. My sister still comes to my readings, and I to hers. We have written a novel together.

In revisiting *for colored girls,* I have made a few changes and additions. Beau Willie is now returning from Iraq. And with the devastation of HIV/AIDS, a clear and present danger particularly to women of color, I felt it would be irresponsible to not address the pandemic and wrote "positive." The other poems, which started out with me in San Francisco and found their way into the mix along the route to New York, remain. As you read, feel free to speak the words aloud. In the mists and fog of life find your way to the rainbow by the sound of your own voice.

When I set out three decades ago for New York, I never realized what *for colored girls* was destined to become. I look back now with awe as gray slate clouds, ominous and dense, give way to a pastel prism of color, dancing cross the sky. And I look forward to discovering even more colors to add to the rainbow that is this colored girl's wonderful journey. Now . . . back to the beginning.

Ntozake, July 2010

*The stage is in darkness. Harsh
music is heard as dim blue lights
come up. One after another, seven
women run onto the stage from
each of the exits. They all freeze in
postures of distress. The follow
spot picks up the lady in brown. She
comes to life and looks around at
the other ladies. All of the others
are still. She walks over to the lady
in red and calls to her. The lady
in red makes no response.*

    lady in brown
dark phrases of womanhood
of never havin been a girl
half-notes scattered
without rhythm/ no tune
distraught laughter fallin
over a black girl's shoulder
it's funny/ it's hysterical
the melody-less-ness of her dance
don't tell nobody don't tell a soul
she's dancin on beer cans & shingles

this must be the spook house
another song with no singers
lyrics/ no voices

& interrupted solos
unseen performances

are we ghouls?
children of horror?
the joke?

don't tell nobody don't tell a soul
are we animals? have we gone crazy?

i can't hear anythin
but maddening screams
& the soft strains of death
& you promised me
you promised me . . .
somebody/ anybody
sing a black girl's song
bring her out
to know herself
to know you
but sing her rhythms
carin/ struggle/ hard times
sing her song of life
she's been dead so long
closed in silence so long
she doesn't know the sound
of her own voice
her infinite beauty

she's half-notes scattered
without rhythm/ no tune
sing her sighs
sing the song of her possibilities
sing a righteous gospel
let her be born
let her be born
& handled warmly.

    lady in brown
i'm outside chicago

    lady in yellow
i'm outside detroit

    lady in purple
i'm outside houston

    lady in red
i'm outside baltimore

    lady in green
i'm outside san francisco

    lady in blue
i'm outside manhattan

    lady in orange
i'm outside st. louis

lady in brown
& this is for colored girls who have considered suicide
but moved to the ends of their own rainbows.

  everyone
mama's little baby likes shortnin, shortnin,
mama's little baby likes shortnin bread
mama's little baby likes shortnin, shortnin,
mama's little baby likes shortnin bread

little sally walker, sittin in a saucer
rise, sally, rise, wipe your weepin eyes
an put your hands on your hips
an let your backbone slip
o, shake it to the east
o, shake it to the west
shake it to the one
that you like the best

  lady in purple
you're it

> As the lady in brown tags each of
> the other ladies they freeze. When
> each one has been tagged the lady
> in brown freezes. Immediately
> "Dancing in the Street" by Martha
> and the Vandellas is heard. All

of the ladies start to dance. The
lady in green, the lady in blue, and
the lady in yellow do the pony,
the big boss line, the swim, and
the nose dive. The other ladies
dance in place.

    lady in yellow
it was graduation nite & i waz the only virgin in the crowd
bobby mills martin jerome & sammy yates eddie jones & randi
all cousins
all the prettiest niggers in this factory town
carried me out wit em
in a deep black buick
smellin of thunderbird & ladies in heat
we rambled from camden to mount holly
laughin at the afternoon's speeches
& danglin our tassles from the rear view mirror
climbin different sorta project stairs
movin toward snappin beer cans &
GET IT GET IT THAT'S THE WAY TO DO IT MAMA
all mercer county graduated the same nite
        cosmetology secretarial pre-college autoshop & business
all us movin from mama to what ever waz out there

that nite we raced a big ol truck from the barbeque stand
trying to tell him bout the party at jacqui's
where folks graduated last year waz waitin to hit it wid us

i got drunk & cdnt figure out
whose hand waz on my thigh/ but it didn't matter
cuz these cousins martin eddie sammy jerome & bobby
waz my sweethearts alternately since the seventh grade
& everybody knew i always started cryin if somebody actually
tried to take advantage of me
        at jacqui's
ulinda mason was stickin her mouth all out
while we tumbled out the buick
eddie jones waz her lickin stick
but i knew how to dance
        it got soo hot
vincent ramos puked all in the punch
& harly jumped all in tico's face
cuz he was leavin for the navy in the mornin
hadda kick ass so we'd all remember how bad he waz
seems like sheila & marguerite waz fraid
to get their hair turnin back
so they laid up against the wall
lookin almost sexy
didnt wanna sweat
but me & my fellas   we waz dancin

since 1963 i'd won all kinda contests
wid the cousins at the POLICE ATHLETIC LEAGUE DANCES
all mercer county knew
any kin to martin yates cd turn somersaults
fore smokey robinson cd get a woman excited

22/

The Dells singing "Stay" is heard

we danced   doin nasty ol tricks

> *The lady in yellow sings along*
> *with the Dells for a moment. The*
> *lady in orange and the lady in blue*
> *jump up and parody the lady in*
> *yellow and the Dells. The lady in*
> *yellow stares at them. They sit down.*

doin nasty ol tricks i'd been thinkin since may
cuz graduation nite had to be hot
& i waz the only virgin
so i hadda make like my hips waz inta some business
that way everybody thot whoever was gettin it
was a older man cdnt run tho streets wit youngsters
martin slipped his leg round my thigh
the dells bumped "stay"
up & down—up & down the new carver homes
WE WAZ GROWN   WE WAZ FINALLY GROWN

ulinda alla sudden went crazy
went over to eddie cursin & carryin on
tearin his skin wid her nails
the cousins tried to talk sense to her
tried to hold her arms
lissin bitch sammy went on

bobby whispered i shd go wit him
fore they go ta cuttin
fore the police arrived
we teetered silently thru the parkin lot
no un uhuh
we didn't know nothin bout no party
bobby started lookin at me
yeah
he started looking at me real strange
like i waz a woman or somethin/
started talkin real soft
in the backseat of that ol buick
WOW
by daybreak
i just cdnt stop grinnin.

*The Dells singing "Stay" comes in
and all of the ladies except the lady
in blue join in and sing along.*

   lady in blue
you gave it up in a buick?

   lady in yellow
yeh, and honey, it was wonderful.

   lady in green
we used to do it all up in the dark
in the corners . . .

lady in blue
some niggah sweating all over you.

lady in red
it was good!

lady in blue
i never did like to grind.

lady in yellow
what other kind of dances are there?

lady in blue
mambo, bomba, merengue

when i waz sixteen i ran off to the south bronx
cuz i waz gonna meet up wit willie colon
& dance all the time
                         mamba bomba merengue
lady in yellow
do you speak spanish?

lady in blue
olà
my papa thot he was puerto rican & we wda been
cept we waz just reglar niggahs wit hints of spanish
so off i made it to this 36 hour marathon dance
con salsa con ricardo
'suggggggggggar' ray on southern blvd

next door to this fotografi place
jammed wit burial weddin & communion relics
next door to la real ideal genuine spanish barber
             up up up up up stairs & stairs & lotsa hallway
wit my colored new jersey self
didn't know what anybody waz saying
cept if dancin waz proof of origin
        i was jibarita herself that nite
& the next day
i kept smilin & right on steppin
if he cd lead i waz ready to dance
if he cdnt lead
i caught this attitude
      i'd seen rosa do
& wd not be bothered
i waz twirlin hippin givin much quik feet
& bein a mute cute colored puerto rican
til saturday afternoon when the disc-jockey say
'SORRY FOLKS WILLIE COLON AINT GONNA MAKE IT TODAY'
& alla my niggah temper came outta control
& i wdnt dance wit nobody
& i talked english loud
& i love you more than i waz mad
uh huh uh huh
more than more than
when i discovered archie shepp & subtle blues
doncha know i wore out the magic of juju
heroically resistin being possessed

ooooooooooooooh the sounds
sneakin in under age to slug's
to stare ata real 'artiste'
& every word outta imamu's mouth waz gospel
& if jesus cdnt play a horn like shepp
waznt no need for colored folks to bear no cross at all

& poem is my thank-you for music
& i love you more than poem
more than aureliano buendia loved macondo
more than hector lavoe loved himself
more than the lady loved gardenias
more than celia loves cuba or graciela loves el son
more than the flamingoes shoo-do-n-doo-wah love bein pretty

oyè négro
te amo mas que   te amo mas que
when you play
yr flute

    everyone (very softly)
te amo mas que   te amo mas que

    lady in red
without any assistance or guidance from you
i have loved you assiduously for 8 months 2 wks & a day
i have been stood up four times
i've left 7 packages on yr doorstep

forty poems 2 plants & 3 handmade notecards i left
town so i cd send to you have been no help to me
on my job
you call at 3:00 in the mornin on weekdays
so i cd drive 27½ miles cross the bay before i go to work
charmin charmin
but you are of no assistance
i want you to know
this waz an experiment
to see how selfish i cd be
if i wd really carry on to snare a possible lover
if i waz capable of debasin my self for the love of another
if i cd stand not being wanted
when i wanted to be wanted
& i cannot
so
with no further assistance & no guidance from you
i am endin this affair

this note is attached to a plant
i've been waterin since the day i met you
you may water it
yr damn self

    lady in orange
i dont wanna write
in english or spanish
i wanna sing   make you dance
like the bata   dance   scream

twitch hips wit me cuz
i done forgot all abt words
aint got no definitions
i wanna whirl
           with you

                    Music starts, "Che Che Cole" by
                    Willie Colon.
                    Everyone starts to dance.

our whole body
wrapped like a ripe mango
ramblin whippin thru space
on the corner in the park
where the rug useta be
let willie colon take you out
swing your head
push your leg to the moon with me

i'm on the lower east side
in new york city
and i can't   i can't
talk witchu no more

    lady in yellow
we gotta dance to keep from cryin

    lady in brown
we gotta dance to keep from dyin

29/

lady in red
so come on

lady in brown
come on

lady in purple
come on

lady in orange
hold yr head like it was ruby sapphire
i'm a poet
who writes in english
come to share the worlds witchu

everyone
come to share our worlds witchu
we come here to be dancin
       to be dancin
     to be dancin
    baya

> *There is a sudden light change, all of the ladies react as if they had been struck in the face. The lady in green and the lady in yellow run out up left, the lady in orange runs out the left volm, the lady in brown runs out up right.*

lady in blue
a friend is hard to press charges against

lady in red
if you know him
you must have wanted it

lady in purple
a misunderstanding

lady in red
you know
these things happen

lady in blue
are you sure
you didn't suggest

lady in purple
had you been drinkin

lady in red
a rapist is always to be a stranger
to be legitimate
someone you never saw
a man wit obvious problems

lady in purple
pin-ups attached to the insides of his lapels

lady in blue
ticket stubs from porno flicks in his pocket

lady in purple
a lil dick

lady in red
or a strong mother

lady in blue
or just a brutal virgin

lady in red
but if you've been seen in public wit him
danced one dance
kissed him good-bye lightly

lady in purple
wit closed mouth

lady in blue
pressin charges will be as hard
as keepin yr legs closed
while five fools try to run a train on you

lady in red
these men friends of ours
who smile nice

stay employed
and take us out to dinner

 lady in purple
lock the door behind you

 lady in blue
wit fist in face
to fuck

 lady in red
who make elaborate mediterranean dinners
& let the art ensemble carry all ethical burdens
while they invite a coupla friends over to have you
are sufferin from latent rapist bravado
& we arc left wit the scars

 lady in blue
bein betrayed by mcn who know us

 lady in purple
& expect
like the stranger
we always thot waz comin

 lady in blue
that we will submit

lady in purple
we must have known

lady in red
women relinquish all personal rights
in the presence of a man
who apparently cd be considered a rapist

lady in purple
especially if he has been considered a friend

lady in blue
& is no less worthy of bein beat witin an inch of his life
bein publicly ridiculed
havin two fists shoved up his ass

lady in red
than the stranger
we always thot it wd be

lady in blue
who never showed up

lady in red
cuz it turns out the nature of rape has changed

lady in blue
we can now meet them in circles we frequent for companionship

> *lady in purple*
we see them at the coffeehouse

> *lady in blue*
wit someone else we know

> *lady in red*
we cd even have em over for dinner
& get raped in our own houses
by invitation
a friend

> > *The lights change, and the ladies*
> > *are all hit by an imaginary slap, the*
> > *lady in red runs off up left.*

> *lady in blue*
eyes

> *lady in purple*
mice

> *lady in blue*
womb

> *lady in blue and lady in purple*
nobody

> > *The lady in purple exits up right.*

lady in blue
tubes tables white washed windows
grime from age wiped over once
legs spread
anxious
eyes crawling up on me
eyes rollin in my thighs
metal horses gnawin my womb
dead mice fall from my mouth
i really didnt mean to
i really didnt think i cd
just one day off . . .
get offa me alla this blood
bones shattered like soft ice-cream cones

i cdnt have people
lookin at me
pregnant
i cdnt have my friends see this
dyin danglin tween my legs
& i didnt say a thing
not a sigh
or a fast scream
to get
those eyes offa me
get them steel rods outta me
this hurts
this hurts me

& nobody came
cuz nobody knew
once i waz pregnant & shamed of myself.

> *The lady in blue exits stage left*
> *volm.*

> *Soft deep music is heard, voices*
> *calling "Sechita" come from the*
> *wings and volms. The lady in*
> *purple enters from up right.*

    lady in purple
once there were quadroon halls/ elegance in st. louis/ lacod
mulattoes/ gamblin down the mississippi/ to memphis/ new
orleans n okra crepes near the bayou/ where the poor white trash
wd sing/ moanin/ strange/ liquid tones/ thru the swamps/

> *The lady in green enters from the*
> *right volm; she is Sechita and for*
> *the rest of the poem dances out*
> *Sechita's life.*

sechita had heard these things/ she moved
as if she'd known them/ the silver n high-toned laughin/
the violins n marble floors/ sechita pushed the clingin
delta dust wit painted toes/ the patch-work tent waz
poka-dotted/ stale lights snatched at the shadows/ creole

carnival waz playin natchez in ten minutes/ her splendid
red garters/ gin-stained n itchy on her thigh/ blk-diamond
stockings darned wit yellow threads/ an ol starched taffeta
can-can fell abundantly orange/ from her waist round the
splinterin chair/ sechita/ egyptian/ goddess of creativity/
2nd millennium/ threw her heavy hair in a coil over her neck/
sechita/ goddess/ the recordin of history/ spread crimson oil
on her cheeks/ waxed her eyebrows/ n unconsciously slugged
the last hard whiskey in the glass/ the broken mirror she
used to decorate her face/ made her forehead tilt backwards/
her cheeks appear sunken/ her sassy chin only large enuf/
to keep her full lower lip/ from growin into her neck/ sechita/
had learned to make allowances for the distortions/
but the heavy dust of the delta/ left a tinge of grit n
darkness/ on every one of her dresses/ on her arms & her
shoulders/ sechita/ waz anxious to get back to st. louis/
the dirt there didnt crawl from the earth into yr soul/
at least/ in st. louis/ the grime waz store bought
second-hand/ here in natchez/ god seemed to be wipin his
feet in her face/

one of the wrestlers had finally won
tonite/ the mulatto/ raul/ was sposed to hold the boomin
half-caste/ searin eagle/ in a bear hug/ 8 counts/ get
thrown unawares/ fall out the ring/ n then do searin eagle
in for good/ sechita/ cd hear redneck whoops n slappin on
the back/ she gathered her sparsely sequined skirts/ tugged
the waist cincher from under her greyin slips/ n made her face

immobile/ she made her face like nefertiti/ approachin her
own tomb/ she suddenly threw/ her leg full-force/ thru the
canvas curtain/ a deceptive glass stone/ sparkled/ malignant
on her ankle/ her calf waz tauntin in the brazen carnie
lights/ the full moon/ sechita/ goddess/ of love/ egypt/
2nd millennium/ performin the rites/ the conjurin of men/
conjurin the spirit/ in natchez/ the mississippi spewed
a heavy fume of barely movin waters/ sechita's legs slashed
furiously thru the cracker nite/ & gold pieces hittin the
makeshift stage/ her thighs/ they were aimin coins tween her
thighs/ sechita/ egypt/ goddess/ harmony/ kicked viciously
thru the nite/ catchin stars tween her toes.

*The lady in green exits into the
stage left volm, the lady in purple
exits into up stage left.*

*The lady in brown enters from up
stage right.*

lady in brown
de library waz right down from de trolly tracks
cross from de laundry-mat
thru de big shinin floors & granite pillars
ol st. louis is famous for
i found toussaint
but not til after months uv
cajun katie/ pippi longstockin

christopher robin/ eddie heyward & a pooh bear
in the children's room
only pioneer girls & magic rabbits
& big city white boys
i knew i waznt sposedta
but i ran inta the ADULT READING ROOM
         & came across

     TOUSSAINT

       my first blk man
(i never counted george washington carver
cuz i didnt like peanuts)
       still
TOUSSAINT waz a blk man a negro like my mama say
who refused to be a slave
& he spoke french
& didnt low no white man to tell him nothin
      not napoleon
      not maximillien
      not robespierre

TOUSSAINT L'OUVERTURE
waz the beginnin uv reality for me
in the summer contest for
who colored child can read
15 books in three weeks
i won & raved abt TOUSSAINT L'OUVERTURE
at the afternoon ceremony

40/

waz disqualified
      cuz Toussaint
         belonged in the ADULT READING ROOM
         & i cried
& carried dead Toussaint home in the book
he waz dead & livin to me
cuz TOUSSAINT & them
they held the citadel gainst the french
wid the spirits of ol dead africans from outta the ground
TOUSSAINT led they army of zombies
walkin cannon ball shootin spirits to free Haiti
& they waznt slaves no more

        TOUSSAINT L'OUVERTURE
became my secret lover at the age of 8
i entertained him in my bedroom
widda flashlight under my covers
way inta the night/ we discussed strategies
how to remove white girls from my hopscotch games
& etc.
TOUSSAINT
waz layin in bed wit me next to raggedy ann
the night i decided to run away from my
        integrated home
         integrated street
         integrated school
1955 waz not a good year for lil blk girls

Toussaint said 'lets go to haiti'

i said 'awright'
& packed some very important things in a brown paper bag
so i wdnt haveta come back
then Toussaint & i took the hodiamont streetcar
to the river
last stop
only 15¢
cuz there waznt nobody cd see Toussaint cept me
& we walked all down thru north st. louis
where the french settlers usedta live
in tiny brick houses all huddled together
wit barely missin windows & shingles uneven
wit colored kids playin & women on low porches sippin beer

i cd talk to Toussaint down by the river
like this waz where we waz gonna stow away
on a boat for new orleans
& catch a creole fishin-rig for port-au-prince
then we waz just gonna read & talk all the time
& eat fried bananas
                  we waz just walkin & skippin past ol drunk men
when dis ol young boy jumped out at me sayin
'HEY GIRL YA BETTAH COME OVAH HEAH N TALK TO ME'
well
i turned to TOUSSAINT (who waz furious)
& i shouted
'ya silly ol boy
ya bettah leave me alone

or TOUSSAINT'S gonna get yr ass'
de silly ol boy came round de corner laughin all in my face
'yellah gal
ya sure must be somebody to know my name so quick'
i waz disgusted
& wanted to get on to haiti
widout some tacky ol boy botherin me
still he kept standin there
kickin milk cartons & bits of brick
tryin to get all in my business
                    i mumbled to L'OUVERTURE 'what shd I do'
finally
i asked this silly ol boy
'WELL WHO ARE YOU?'
he say
'MY NAME IS TOUSSAINT JONES'
well
i looked right at him
those skidded out corduroy pants
a striped teashirt wid holes in both elbows
a new scab over his left eye
& i said
                    'what's yr name again'
he say
'i'm toussaint jones'
'wow
i am on my way to see
TOUSSAINT L'OUVERTURE in HAITI

are ya any kin to him
he dont take no stuff from no white folks
& they gotta country all they own
& there aint no slaves'
that silly ol boy squinted his face all up
'looka heah girl
i am TOUSSAINT JONES
& i'm right heah lookin at ya
& i dont take no stuff from no white folks
ya dont see none round heah do ya?'
& he sorta pushed out his chest
then he say
'come on   lets go on down to the docks
& look at the boats'
i waz real puzzled goin down to the docks
wit my paper bag & my books
i felt TOUSSAINT L'OUVERTURE sorta leave me
& i waz sad
til i realized
TOUSSAINT JONES waznt too different
from TOUSSAINT L'OUVERTURE
cept the ol one waz in haiti
& this one wid me speakin english & eatin apples
yeah.
toussaint jones waz awright wit me
no tellin what all spirits we cd move
down by the river
st. louis 1955   hey wait.

*The lady in brown exits into the
stage right volm.*

*The lady in red enters from the
stage left volm.*

    lady in red
orange butterflies & aqua sequins
ensconsed tween slight bosoms
silk roses dartin from behind her ears
the passion flower of southwest los angeles
meandered down hoover street
past dark shuttered houses where
women from louisiana shelled peas
round 3:00 & sent their sons
whistlin to the store for fatback & black-eyed peas
she glittered in heat
& seemed to be lookin for rides
when she waznt & absolutely
eyed every man who waznt lame white or noddin out
she let her thigh slip from her skirt
crossin the street
she slowed to be examined
& she never looked back to smile
or acknowledge a sincere 'hey mama'
or to meet the eyes of someone
purposely findin sometin to do in

her direction
        she waz sullen
        & the rhinestones etchin the corners of her mouth
        suggested tears
        fresh kisses that had done no good
she always wore her stomach out
lined with small iridescent feathers
the hairs round her navel seemed to dance
& she didnt let on
she knew
from behind her waist waz aching to be held
the pastel ivy drawn on her shoulders
to be brushed with lips & fingers
smellin of honey & jack daniels
        she waz hot
        a deliberate coquette
        who never did without
        what she wanted
& she wanted to be unforgettable
she wanted to be a memory
a wound   to every man
arragant enough to want her
        she waz the wrath
       of women in windows
          fingerin shades/ ol lace curtains
         camoflagin despair &
         stretch marks
so she glittered honestly

delighted she waz desired
& allowed those especially
schemin/ tactful suitors
to experience her body & spirit
tearin/ so easily blendin with theirs/
& they were so happy
& lay on her lime sheets full & wet
from her tongue   she kissed
them reverently   even ankles
edges of beards . . .

The stage goes to darkness except
for a special on the lady in red,
who lies motionless on the floor; as
the lights slowly fade up the lady
in red sits up.

at 4:30 AM
she rose
movin the arms & legs that trapped her
she sighed affirmin the sculptured man
& made herself a bath
of dark musk oil egyptian crystals
& florida water to remove his smell
to wash away the glitter
to watch the butterflies melt into
suds & the rhinestones fall beneath
her buttocks like smooth pebbles

in a missouri creek
layin in water
she became herself
ordinary
brown braided woman
with big legs & full lips
reglar
seriously intendin to finish her
night's work
she quickly walked to her guest
straddled on her pillows & began
        'you'll have to go now/ i've
        a lot of work to do/ & i cant
        with a man around/ here are yr pants/
        there's coffee on the stove/ its been
        very nice/ but i cant see you again/
        you got what you came for/ didnt you'
& she smiled
he wd either mumble curses bout crazy bitches
or sit dumbfounded
while she repeated
        'i cdnt possibly wake up/ with
        a strange man in my bed/ why
        dont you go home'
she cda been slapped upside the head
or verbally challenged
but she never waz
& the ones who fell prey to the

dazzle of hips painted with
orange blossoms & magnolia scented wrists
had wanted no more
than to lay between her sparklin thighs
& had planned on leavin before dawn
& she had been so divine
devastatingly bizarre the way
her mouth fit round
& now she stood a
reglar colored girl
fulla the same malice
livid indifference as a sistah
worn from supportin a wd be hornplayer
or waitin by the window

         & they knew
         & left in a hurry

she wd gather her tinsel &
jewels from the tub
& laugh gayly or vengeful
she stored her silk roses by her bed
& when she finished writin
the account of her exploit in a diary
embroidered with lilies & moonstones
she placed the rose behind her ear
& cried herself to sleep.

    lady in blue
i usedta live in the world
then i moved to HARLEM
& my universe is now six blocks

when i walked in the pacific
i imagined waters ancient from accra/ tunis
cleansin me/ feedin me
now my ankles are coated in grey filth
from the puddle neath the hydrant

my oceans were life
what waters i have here sit stagnant
circlin ol men's bodies
shit & broken lil whiskey bottles
left to make me bleed

i usedta live in the world
now i live in harlem & my universe is six blocks
a tunnel with a train
i can ride anywhere
remaining a stranger

NO MAN YA CANT GO WITH ME/ I DONT EVEN
KNOW YOU/ NO/ I DONT WANNA KISS YOU/
YOU AINT BUT 12 YRS OLD/ NO MAN/ PLEASE
PLEASE PLEASE LEAVE ME ALONE/ TOMORROW/ YEAH/
NO/ PLEASE/ I CANT USE IT

    i cd stay alone
    a woman in the world
    then i moved to
HARLEM
i come in at dusk
stay close to the curb

> *The lady in yellow enters, she's*
> *waiting for a bus.*

round midnite
praying wont no young man
think i'm pretty in a dark mornin

> *The lady in purple enters, she's*
> *waiting for a bus.*

wdnt be good
not good at all
to meet a tall short black brown young man fulla his power
in the dark
in my universe of six blocks
straight up brick walls
women hangin outta windows

like ol silk stockings
cats cryin/ children gigglin/ a tavern wit red curtains
bad smells/ kissin ladies smilin & dirt
sidewalks spittin/ men cursing/ playin

The lady in orange enters, she is
being followed by a man, the
lady in blue becomes that man.

'I SPENT MORE MONEY YESTERDAY
THAN THE DAY BEFORE & ALL THAT'S MORE N YOU
NIGGAH EVER GOTTA HOLD TO
COME OVER HERE BITCH
CANT YA SEE THIS IS $5'

never mind sister
dont pay him no mind
go go go go go go sister
do yr thing
never mind

i usedta live in the world
really be in the world
free & sweet talkin
good mornin & thank-you & nice day
uh huh
i cant now
i cant be nice to nobody

nice is such a rip-off
reglar beauty & a smile in the street
is just a set-up

i usedta be in the world
a woman in the world
i hadda right to the world
then i moved to harlem
for the set-up
a universe
six blocks of cruelty
piled up on itself
a tunnel
closin

*The four ladies on stage freeze,
count 4, then the ladies in
blue, purple, yellow, and orange
move to their places for the next
poem.*

　　　lady in purple
three of us like a pyramid
three friends
one laugh
one music
one flowered shawl
knotted on each neck

we all saw him at the same time
& he saw us
i felt a quick thump in each one of us
didnt know what to do
we all wanted what waz comin our way
so we split
but he found one
& she loved him

the other two were tickled
& spurned his advances
when the one who loved him waz somewhere else
he wd come to her saying
yr friends love you very much
i have tried
& they keep askin where are you
she smiled
wonderin how long her friends
wd hold out
he waz what they were lookin for
he bided his time
he waited til romance waned
the three of us made up stories
bout usedta & cda been nice
the season waz dry
no men
no quickies
not one dance or eyes unrelentin

one day after another
cept for the one who loved him
he appeared irregularly
expectin graciousness no matter what
she cut fresh strawberries
her friends callt less frequently
went on hunts for passin fancies
she cdnt figure out what waz happenin
then the rose
she left by his pillow
she found on her friends desk
& there waz nothing to say
she said
i wanna tell you
he's been after me
all the time
says he's free & can explain
what's happenin wit you
is nothin to me
& i dont wanna hurt you
but you know i need someone now
& you know
how wonderful he is

her friend cdnt speak or cry
they hugged & went to where he waz
wit another woman
he said good-bye to one

tol the other he wd call
he smiled a lot

she held her head on her lap
the lap of her sisters soakin up tears
each understandin how much love stood between them
how much love between them
love between them
love like sisters

*Sharp music is heard, each lady
dances as if catching a disease from
the lady next to her, suddenly
they all freeze.*

lady in orange
ever since i realized there waz someone callt
a colored girl an evil woman a bitch or a nag
i been tryin not to be that & leave bitterness
in somebody else's cup/ come to somebody to love me
without deep & nasty smellin scald from lye or bein
left screamin in a street fulla lunatica/ whisperin
slut bitch bitch niggah/ get outta here wit alla that/
i didnt have any of that for you/ i brought you what joy
i found & i found joy/ honest fingers round my face/ with
dead musicians on 78's from cuba/ or live musicians on five
dollar lp's from chicago/ where i have never been/ & i love
willie colon & arsenio rodriguez/ especially cuz i can make

the music loud enuf/ so there is no me but dance/ & when
i can dance like that/ there's nothin cd hurt me/ but
i get tired & i haveta come offa the floor & then there's
that woman who hurt you/ who you left/ three or four times/
& just went back/ after you put my heart in the bottom of
yr shoe/ you just walked back to where you hurt/ & i didnt
have nothin/ so i went to where somebody had somethin for me/
but he waznt you/ & i waz on the way back from her house
in the bottom of yr shoe/ so this is not a love poem/ cuz there
are only memorial albums available/ & even charlie mingus
wanted desperately to be a pimp/ & i wont be able to see eddie
palmieri for months/ so this is a requium for myself/ cuz i
have died in a real way/ not wid aqua coffins & du-wop cadillacs/
i used to joke abt when i waz messin round/ but a real dead
lovin is here for you now/ cuz i dont know anymore/ how
to avoid my own face wet wit my tears/ cuz i had convinced
myself colored girls had no right to sorrow/ & i lived
& loved that way & kept sorrow on the curb/ allegedly
for you/ but i know i did it for myself/
i cdnt stand it
i cdnt stand bein sorry & colored at the same time
it's so redundant in the modern world

   lady in purple
i lived wit myths & music waz my ol man & i cd dance
a dance outta time/ a dance wit no partners/ take my
pills & keep right on steppin/ linger in non-english
speakin arms so there waz no possibility of understandin

& you YOU
came sayin i am the niggah/ i am the baddest muthafuckah
out there/
i said yes/ this is who i am waitin for
& to come wit you/ i hadta bring everythin
the dance & the terror
the dead musicians & the hope
& those scars i had hidden wit smiles & good fuckin
lay open
& i dont know i dont know any more tricks
i am really colored & really sad sometimes & you hurt me
more than i ever danced outta/ into oblivion isnt far enuf
to get outta this/ i am ready to die like a lily in the
desert/ & i cdnt let you in on it cuz i didnt know/ here
is what i have/ poems/ big thighs/ lil tits/ &
so much love/ will you take it from me this one time/
please this is for you/ arsenio's tres cleared the way
& makes me pure again/ please please/ this is for you
i want you to love me/ let me love you/ i dont wanna
dance wit ghosts/ snuggle lovers i made up in my drunkenness/
lemme love you just like i am/ a colored girl/ i'm finally bein
real/ no longer symmetrical & impervious to pain

   lady in blue
we deal wit emotion too much
so why dont we go on ahead & be white then/
& make everythin dry & abstract wit no rhythm & no
reelin for sheer sensual pleasure/ yes let's go on

& be white/ we're right in the middle of it/ no use
holdin out/ holdin onto ourselves/ lets think our
way outta feelin/ lets abstract ourselves some families
& maybe maybe tonite/ i'll find a way to make myself
come without you/ no fingers or other objects just thot
which isnt spiritual evolution cuz its empty & godliness
is plenty is ripe & fertile/ thinkin wont do me a bit of
good tonite/ i need to be loved/ & havent the audacity
to say
where are you/ & dont know who to say it to

   lady in yellow
i've lost it
touch wit reality/ i dont know who's doin it
i thot i waz but i waz so stupid i waz able to be hurt
& that's not real/ not anymore/ i shd be immune/ if i'm
still alive & that's what i waz discussin/ how i am still
alive & my dependency on other livin beins for love
i survive on intimacy & tomorrow/ that's all i've got goin
& the music waz like smack & you knew abt that
& still refused my dance waz not enuf/ & it waz all i had
but bein alive & bein a woman & bein colored is a metaphysical
dilemma/ i havent conquered yet/ do you see the point
my spirit is too ancient to understand the separation of
soul & gender/ my love is too delicate to have thrown
back on my face

> *The ladies in red, green, and brown*
> *enter quietly; in the background*
> *all of the ladies except the lady in*
> *yellow are frozen; the lady in*
> *yellow looks at them, walks by*
> *them, touches them; they do not*
> *move.*

    lady in yellow
my love is too delicate to have thrown back on my face

> *The lady in yellow starts to exit*
> *into the stage right volm. Just as she*
> *gets to the volm, the lady in brown*
> *comes to life.*

    lady in brown
my love is too beautiful to have thrown back on my face

    lady in purple
my love is too sanctified to have thrown back on my face

    lady in blue
my love is too magic to have thrown back on my face

    lady in orange
my love is too saturday nite to have thrown back on my face

    lady in red
my love is too complicated to have thrown back on my face

    lady in green
my love is too music to have thrown back on my face

    everyone
music
music

> *The lady in green then breaks into*
> *a dance, the other ladies follow*
> *her lead and soon they are all danc-*
> *ing and chanting together.*

    lady in green
yank dankka dank dank

    everyone
music

    lady in green
yank dankka dank dank

    everyone
music

    lady in green
yank dankka dank dank

everyone (but started by the lady in yellow)
delicate
delicate
delicate

everyone (but started by the lady in brown)
and beautiful
and beautiful
and beautiful

everyone (but started by the lady in purple)
oh sanctified
oh sanctified
oh sanctified

everyone (but started by the lady in blue)
magic
magic
magic

everyone (but started by the lady in orange)
and saturday nite
and saturday nite
and saturday nite

everyone (but started by the lady in red)
and complicated
and complicated

and complicated

and complicated

and complicated

and complicated

and complicated

and complicated

*The dance reaches a climax and all
of the ladies fall out tired, but full
of life and togetherness.*

    lady in green
somebody almost walked off wid alla my stuff

not my poems or a dance i gave up in the street

but somebody almost walked off wid alla my stuff

like a kleptomaniac workin hard & forgettin while stealin

this is mine/ this aint yr stuff/

now why dont you put me back & let me hang out in my own self

somebody almost walked off wid alla my stuff

& didnt care enuf to send a note home sayin

i waz late for my solo conversation

or two sizes too small for my own tacky skirts

what can anybody do wit somethin of no value on

a open market/ did you getta dime for my things/

hey man/ where are you goin wid alla my stuff/

this is a woman's trip & i need my stuff/

to ohh & ahh abt/ daddy/ i gotta mainline number

from my own shit/ now wontchu put me back/ & let

me play this duet/ wit this silver ring in my nose/
honest to god/ somebody almost run off wit alla my stuff/
& i didnt bring anythin but the kick & sway of it
the perfect ass for my man & none of it is theirs
this is mine/ ntozake 'her own things'/ that's my name/
now give me my stuff/ i see ya hidin my laugh/ & how i
sit wif my legs open sometimes/ to give my crotch
some sunlight/ & there goes my love my toes my chewed
up finger nails/ niggah/ wif the curls in yr hair/
mr. louisiana hot link/ i want my stuff back/
my rhythms & my voice/ open my mouth/ & let me talk ya
outta/ throwin my shit in the sewar/ this is some delicate
leg & whimsical kiss/ i gotta have to give to my choice/
without you runnin off wit alla my shit/
now you cant have me less i give me away/ & i waz
doin all that/ til ya run off on a good thing/
who is this you left me wit/ some simple bitch
widda bad attitude/ i wants my things/
i want my arm wit the hot iron scar/ & my leg wit the
flea bite/ i want my calloused feet & quik language back
in my mouth/ fried plantains/ pineapple pear juice/
sun-ra & joseph & jules/ i want my own things/ how i lived them/
& give me my memories/ how i waz when i waz there/
you cant have them or do nothin wit them/
stealin my shit from me/ dont make it yrs/ makes it stolen/
somebody almost run off wit alla my stuff/ & i waz standin
there/ lookin at myself/ the whole time
& it waznt a spirit took my stuff/ waz a man whose

ego walked round like Rodan's shadow/ waz a man faster
n my innocence/ waz a lover/ i made too much
room for/ almost run off wit alla my stuff/
& i didnt know i'd give it up so quik/ & the one running wit it/
dont know he got it/ & i'm shoutin this is mine/ & he dont
know he got it/ my stuff is the anonymous ripped off treasure
of the year/ did you know somebody almost got away with me/
me in a plastic bag under their arm/ me
danglin on a string of personal carelessness/ i'm spattered wit
mud & city rain/ & no i didnt get a chance to take a douche/
hey man/ this is not your perogative/ i gotta have me in my
pocket/ to get round like a good woman shd/ & make the poem
in the pot or the chicken in the dance/ what i got to do/
i gotta have my stuff to do it to/
why dont ya find yr own things/ & leave this package
of me for my destiny/ what ya got to get from me/
i'll give it to ya/ yeh/ i'll give it to ya/
round 5:00 in the winter/ when the sky is blue-red/
& Dew City is gettin pressed/ if it's really my stuff/
ya gotta give it to me/ if ya really want it/ i'm
the only one/ can handle it

　lady in blue
that niggah will be back tomorrow, sayin 'i'm sorry'

　lady in yellow
get this, last week my ol man came in sayin, 'i don't know
how she got yr number baby, i'm sorry'

lady in brown
no this one is it, 'o baby, ya know i was high, i'm sorry'

lady in purple
'i'm only human, and inadequacy is what makes us human, &
if we was perfect we wdnt have nothin to strive for, so you
might as well go on and forgive me pretty baby, cause i'm sorry'

lady in green
'shut up bitch, i told you i waz sorry'

lady in orange
no this one is it, 'i do ya like i do ya cause i thot
ya could take it, now i'm sorry'

lady in red
'now i know that ya know i love ya, but i aint ever gonna
love ya like ya want me to love ya, i'm sorry'

lady in blue
one thing i dont need
is any more apologies
i got sorry greetin me at my front door
you can keep yrs
i dont know what to do wit em
they dont open doors
or bring the sun back
they dont make me happy

or get a mornin paper
didnt nobody stop usin my tears to wash cars
cuz a sorry

i am simply tired
of collectin
        'i didnt know
        i was so important to you'
i'm gonna haveta throw some away
i cant get to the clothes in my closet
for alla the sorries
i'm gonna tack a sign to my door
leave a message by the phone
        'if you called
        to say yr sorry
        call somebody
        else
        i dont use em anymore'
i let sorry/ didnt meanta/ & how cd i know abt that
take a walk down a dark & musty street in brooklyn
i'm gonna do exactly what i want to
& i wont be sorry for none of it
letta sorry soothe yr soul/ i'm gonna soothe mine

you were always inconsistent
doin somethin & then bein sorry
beatin my heart to death
talkin bout you sorry

well
i will not call
i'm not goin to be nice
i will raise my voice
& scream & holler
& break things & race the engine
& tell all yr secrets bout yrself to yr face
& i will list in detail everyone of my wonderful lovers
& their ways
i will play oliver lake
loud
& i wont be sorry for none of it

i loved you on purpose
i was open on purpose
i still crave vulnerability & close talk
& i'm not even sorry bout you bein sorry
you can carry all the guilt & grime ya wanna
just dont give it to me
i cant use another sorry
next time
you should admit
you're mean/ low-down/ triflin/ & no count straight out
steada bein sorry alla the time
enjoy bein yrself

lady in red
its not that i don't love him/ not that i never loved him/
its just been so many years

lady in yellow
#7QYG9

lady in purple
it's been so many years &/ there/ he was at the concert & he looked the
same way he'd always looked/ & then he looked at me/ the same way he'd
always looked/ & then his arm was around me/
& we walked the same way/ we'd always walked/
& i *fell* into his arms
& we *fell* into the bed

lady in brown
#7QYG9

lady in yellow
it was just the same/ like it had always been/ & I loved him like I'd
always loved him/ it'd been years/ & one by one my clothing *fell* off/ &
little by little he entered me

lady in purple
#7QYG9

lady in brown
& it never occurred to me that there'd been someone else/ even though

it'd been years/ & then we were together again/ & we lived together
again & we loved each other again & I forgot
all the years apart

    lady in red
#7QYG9

    lady in yellow
& we were together/ & then I started making baccalou from scratch/ & I
got a call from carol/ & I said oh come over I'm making baccalou/ & I
said come over we'll have it just for ourselves/ it'll just be us girls/ & we
started giggling & I said this is going to be fun/
& so carol came in all her ashanti robes & her braids

    lady in brown
& her cowrie shells

    lady in yellow
oh my god you look so good

    lady in red
so do you

    lady in yellow
well dj's got me so happy/
i just don't know what to do with myself

    lady in red
& carol said

lady in brown
i don't know why you're so happy, i saw dj & tito hanging out together in front of that bar over on lexington looking more than friendly

lady in purple
& i said

lady in purple and lady in yellow
what

lady in brown
you heard what I said

lady in brown and lady in red
they were together

lady in brown
looking more than friendly

lady in yellow
oh don't be silly/ that's a gay bar & dj 'don't like faggots'/ i have to get on him for calling gay people terrible names/ so he wasn't there unless he was trying to get tito outta there/ but he certainly wasn't there for himself

lady in red
& carol looked at me with a smirk

    lady in purple
& i said

    lady in yellow
you just mind your house n let me tend to mine cause
there's nothing wrong here

    lady in red
& so carol said after awhile

    lady in brown
you know you really need to get tested

    lady in purple and lady in yellow
tested for what?

    lady in red
she said

    lady in red and lady in brown
aids

    lady in purple
i said

    lady in yellow
what in the hell wd i get tested for/
dj & i been together forever

   lady in yellow and lady in red
& she said

   lady in brown
no you've been together for a year/ you were separated forever

   lady in yellow
carol he has been faithful to me for years/ girl you trippin/ i know you're
not suggesting he's on the dl/
ok/ i'm gonna get checked n then i never want to hear any of this from
you again

   lady in purple
after the tone of the lunch had changed we took the train to st. vincents
& the line was long/ we got the blood drawn/
they said it'd be about two weeks before i'd hear anything

   lady in yellow
& I knew I waznt going to hear anything so I just went home & waited
for him to come home & we had a lovely afternoon & finished off the
baccalou

   lady in purple
& finished off me

   lady in yellow
& we had a lovely afternoon &

lady in red
I can't talk about this anymore bcuz I don't have any more energy to
talk about that

lady in yellow
& then I got a telephone call/ & it waz for

lady in brown
#7QYG9

lady in purple
#7QYG9

lady in red
#7QYG9

lady in yellow
& i said I think that's me, but i'm not sick

lady in purple
& i said/ i'm that number but you don't really
want to see me/ there's nothing wrong with me/ & they said

lady in red
let me check your number

lady in purple
so they checked my number/ & they said

lady in red
you tested positive for hiv

lady in purple
& i thought

lady in yellow
i waz gonna faint

lady in brown
how cd I be positive for aids/ I don't take drugs/ am I going to die?

lady in purple
she said

lady in red
oh no you're not going to die/ you're gonna live a full & vigorous life you just have to stay on your meds

lady in purple
& i said

lady in purple and lady in brown
oh ok

lady in yellow
so i went home to wait for dj

lady in red
but he waz already there/ fixin chicken curry

lady in brown
oh, i'm makin you chicken curry

lady in purple
& i said

lady in yellow
i went to the hospital/ & tested positive

lady in red
tested positive?

lady in purple
positive?

lady in brown
positive?

lady in yellow
i tested positive for aids

lady in brown
whadda ya mean you tested positive for aids/ i don't have no goddamn aids/ what are you sayin to me/ that i'm a fuckin faggot/ i didn't give you no goddamn aids/ what you talkin bout/ who have you been sleepin with/ that's what i want to know/ did you give it to me?

lady in purple
& I said/ I gotta believe this test/ i gotta go start treatment on Friday

lady in yellow
fuck that hospital/ get tested again

lady in purple
& I said

lady in yellow
well why don't you come with me & prove to me that you aren't the one
who gave it to me

lady in brown
i ain't going to no goddamn hospital/ you go by urself & get your so called
treatment/ & i ain't been wit no fuckin faggot

lady in yellow
& then there waz silence

lady in red
& his eyes became slits of molten brown

lady in purple
& i saw his left hand clench into something that was dangerous

lady in yellow
& i fell out on the floor/ i don't know what happened/ i was out & when i
started to wake up I rubbed the blood streaming from my eyes & i smelled

burning chicken curry/ I pulled myself up by the stove & i turned the
curry off

    lady in purple
& then i looked around & none of his things were there

    lady in red
his clothes weren't there/ his trinkets weren't there

    lady in yellow
his books weren't there

    lady in brown
everything about him waznt there

    lady in purple
& i waz positive

    lady in yellow
& not positive at all

    ALL
its not that i don't love him/ its not that i never loved him/ it just had
been so many years

    lady in orange
there waz no air/ the sheets made ripples under his
body like crumpled paper napkins in a summer park/ & lil

specks of somethin from tween his toes or the biscuits
from the day before ran I the sweat that tucked the sheets
into his limbs like he waz an ol frozen bundle of chicken/
& he'd get up to make coffee, cook up his crack, drink wine,
drink water/ he wished one of his friends
who knew where he waz wd come by
with some blow or some shit/ anything/ there waz no air/
he'd see the spotlights in the alleyways downstairs movin
in the air/ cross his wall over his face/ like in fallujah & get under the
covers & wait for an all clear or til he cd hear traffic and the children
again/ there waznt nothin wrong with him

   lady in red
there waznt nothing wrong
with him/ p.t.s.d./ p.t.s.c./ p.t.s./ he kept telling crystal
and that social worker/
any niggah wanna kill arab children more n stay home
& raise his own is sicker than a rabid dog/
thats how their thing had gone since he got back/
crystal just got inta sayin whatta fool niggah beau waz
& always had been/ didnt he go all over uptown sayin the
child waznt his/ waz some no counts bastard/ & any ol city
police cd come & get him if they wanted/ cuz as soon as
the blood type & shit waz together/ everybody wd know that
crystal waz a no good lyin whore/ and this after she'd been
his girl since she waz thirteen/ when he caught her
on the stairway

lady in orange
he came home crazy as hell/ he tried to get veterans benefits
for being in Basra an go on to school & they
kept right on putting him in
remedial classes/ he cdnt read wortha damn/
cdnt read Farsi/
cdnt read Arabic/ cdnt read English/
so beau cused the teachers of holdin him back
& got himself
a gypsy cab to drive/ but his cab kept breakin
down/ & the cops waz always
messin with him/ plus not
getting much bread

lady in orange and lady in red
& crystal went & got pregnant again

lady in red
must be that goddamn raghead from the bodega/
beau most beat her to death when she tol him/ she
still gotta scar under her right tit where he cut her up/
still crystal went right on & had the baby/ so now beau willie had
two children/ a little girl/ naomi kenya & a boy/ kwame beau
willie brown/ & there waz no air/
how in the hell did he get in this mess anyway/ somebody
went & tol crystal that beau waz spending alla his money
on the bartendin bitch down at the merry-go-round cafe/
beau sat right up in the bed/ wrapped up in the sheets

lookin like john the Baptist or a huge baby wit stubble
& nuts/ now he hadta get alla that shit outta crystal's
mind/ oh damn/ the pipe waz burnin up his fingers/
his fingers waz turning black just like his teeth
& now his hand waz burnt & he dropped the damn pipe
& he cdnt get outta bed without cutting his feet/ he had to get
her to let him come home/ crystal had gone &
got a court order saying beau willie brown had no access
to his children/ if he showed his face he waz subject
to arrest/ shit/ she'd been in his ass to marry her
since she waz 14 years old & here when she waz 22/ she wanna
throw him out cuz he say he'll marry her/ she burst
out laughin/ hollerin whatchu wanna marry me for now/
so i can support yr
ass/ or come sit wit ya when they lock yr behind
up/ cause they gonna come for ya/ ya goddamn lunatic/
they gonna come/ & i'm not gonna have a thing to do
wit it/ o no i wdnt marry yr pitiful black ass for
nothing & she went to bed/
the next day beau willie came in blasted & got ta swingin
chairs at crystal/ who cdnt figure out what the hell
he waz doin/ til he got ta shoutin bout how she waz gonna
marry him/ & get some more veterans benefits/ & he cd
stop drivin them spics round/ while they tryin
to kill him for $15/ & she cd stop havin Arab children
beau waz sweatin terrible/ member in Basra
beatin on crystal/ & he cdnt do no more with the table n chairs/
so he went to get the high chair/ & lil kwame waz in it/

& beau waz beatin crystal with the high chair & her son/
& some notion got inta him to stop/ and he run out/
crystal most died/ that's why the police wdnt low
beau near where she lived/ & she'd been telling the kids
their daddy tried to kill her & kwame/ & he just wanted
to marry her/ that's what/ he wanted to marry her/ &
have a family/ but the bitch waz crazy/ beau willie
waz sittin in this hotel in his drawers drinkin
coffee, smoking crack, drinking wine
in the heat of the day spillin shit all
over hisself/ laughin/ bout how he waz gonna get crystal
to take him back/ & let him be a man in the house/ & she
wdnt even have to go to work no more/ he got dressed
all up in his ivory shirt & checkered pants to go see
crystal & get this mess all cleared up/
he knocked on the door to crystal's rooms/ & she
didn't answer/ he beat on the door & crystal & naomi
started cryin/ beau got ta shoutin again how he wanted
to marry her/ & waz she always gonna be a whore/ or
did she wanna husband/ & crystal just kept on
screamin for him to leave us alone/ just leave us
alone/ so beau broke the door down/ crystal held
the children in fronta her/ she picked kwame off the
floor/ in her arms/ & she held naomi by her shoulders/
& kept sayin/ beau willie brown/ get outta here/
the police is gonna come for ya/ ya fool/ get outta here/
do you want the children to see you act the fool again/
you want kwame to brain damage from you throwin him

round/ niggah/ get outta here/ get out & don't show yr
ass again or I'll kill ya/
he reached for naomi/ crystal grabbed the lil girl &
stared at beau willie like he waz a leper or something/
don't you touch my children/ muthafucker/ or i'll kill you/
beau willie jumped back all humble & apologetic/ i'm
sorry/ i don't wanna hurt em/ i just wanna hold em &
get on my way/ i don't wanna cuz you no more trouble/
i wanted to marry you & give ya things
what you gonna give/ a broken jaw/ niggah get outta here/
he ignored crystal's outburst & sat down motioning for
naomi to come to him/ she smiled back at her daddy/
crystal felt naomi givin in & held her tighter/
naomi/ pushed away & ran to her daddy/ cryin/ daddy, daddy
come back daddy/ come back/ but be nice to mommy/
cause mommy loves you/ and you gotta be nice/
he sat her on his knee/ & played with her ribbons &
they counted fingers & toes/ every so often he
looked over to crystal holdin kwame/ like a statue/
& he'd say/ see crystal/ I can be a good father/
now let me see my son/ & she didn't move/ &
he coaxed her & he coaxed her/ tol her she waz
still a hot lil ol thing & pretty & strong/ didn't
she get right up after that lil ol fight they had
& go back to work/ beau willie oozed kindness &
crystal who had known so lil/ let beau hold kwame
as soon as crystal let the baby outta her arms/ beau
jumped up a laughin & a giggling/ a hootin & a hollerin/

awright bitch/ awright bitch/ you gonna marry me/
you gonna marry me . . .
i aint gonna marry ya/ I aint ever gonna marry ya/
for nothing/ you gonna be in the jail/ you gonna be
under the jail for this/ now gimme my kids/ ya give
me back my kids/ he kicked the screen outta the window/
& held the kids offa the sill/ you gonna marry me/ yeh, I'll marry ya/
anything/ but bring the children back in the house/
he looked from where the kids were hangin from the
fifth story/ at alla the people screamin at him/ &
he started sweatin like he did in Baghdad/ say it/ say it/ say to alla the
neighbors/ you gonna marry me/
i stood by beau in the window/ with naomi reaching
for me/ & kwame screamin mommy mommy from the fifth
story/ but I cd only whisper/ & he dropped em

    lady in red
i waz missin somethin

    lady in purple
somethin so important

    lady in brown
somethin promised

    lady in blue
a layin on of hands

lady in green
fingers near my forehead

lady in yellow
strong

lady in green
cool

lady in orange
movin

lady in purple
makin me whole

lady in orange
sense

lady in green
pure

lady in blue
all the gods comin into me
layin me open to myself

lady in red
i waz missin somethin

lady in green
somethin promised

lady in orange
somethin free

lady in purple
a layin on of hands

lady in blue
i know bout/ layin on bodies/ layin outta man
bringin him alla my fleshy self & some of my pleasure
bein taken full eager wet like i get sometimes
i waz missin somethin

lady in purple
a layin on of hands

lady in blue
not a man

lady in yellow
layin on

lady in purple
not my mama/ holdin me tight/ sayin
i'm always gonna be her girl
not a layin on of bosom & womb
a layin on of hands
the holiness of myself released

lady in red
i sat up one nite walkin a boardin house
screamin/ cryin/ the ghost of another woman
who waz missin what i waz missin
i wanted to jump up outta my bones
& be done wit myself
leave me alone
& go on in the wind
it waz too much
i fell into a numbness
til the only tree i cd see
took me up in her branches
held me in the breeze
made me dawn dew
that chill at daybreak
the sun wrapped me up swingin rose light everywhere
the sky laid over me like a million men
i waz cold/ i waz burnin up/ a child
& endlessly weavin garments for the moon
wit my tears

i found god in myself
& i loved her/ i loved her fiercely

All of the ladies repeat to them-
selves softly the lines 'i found god
in myself & i loved her.' It soon
becomes a song of joy, started by

the lady in blue. The ladies sing
first to each other, then gradually
to the audience. After the song
peaks the ladies enter into a closed
tight circle.

    lady in brown
& this is for colored girls who have considered
suicide/ but are movin to the ends of their own
rainbows

Ntozake Shange in San Francisco, 1972.

Quantrell Colbert

Kelly (Kerry Washington, *left*), Gilda (Phylicia Rashad, *center*) and Yasmine (Anika Noni Rose, *right*) in *For Colored Girls*.

Quantrell Colbert

Anika Noni Rose stars as Yasmine in *For Colored Girls*.

Loretta Devine stars as Juanita in *For Colored Girls*.

Quantrell Colbert

Quantrell Colbert

Tangie (Thandie Newton, *left*) and Nyla (Tessa Thompson, *right*) in *For Colored Girls*.

91/

Quantrell Colbert

Kimberly Elise stars as Crystal in *For Colored Girls*.

Ntozake Shange and her daughter, Savannah, in the opening scene of the PBS production.

Sarita Allen as Sechita, with Carol Maillard.

93/

Lynn Whitfield with Jack Landron performing the poem "one" in the PBS production.

Laurie Carlos (*second from left*) delivering the lead voice in performance of the poem "i used to live in the world" for the PBS production.

© Rick Tiedemann

Oz Scott, who directed both the PBS production and the Broadway production with Trazana Beverley in preparation for the scene in which "a nite with beau willie brown" is performed.

Courtesy of the author

Ntozake with an original *for colored girl,* Trazana Beverley (*fifth from left*), and the cast of the twenty-fifth-anniversary production of *for colored girls,* which was directed by Ms. Shange and produced by Woodie King Jr. at New York City's Henry Street Settlement/New Federal Theater.

95/

Ntozake Shange with the cast of *for colored girls who have considered suicide/when the rainbow is enuf,* New York, June 11, 1976, *from left*: Rise Collins, Paula Moss, Aku Kadogo, Laurie Carlos, Trazana Beverley, Ntozake Shange, and Janet League. *(Photograph by Richard Avedon © The Richard Avedon Foundation)*

Reading Group Guide
for colored girls who have considered suicide/when the rainbow is enuf
Ntozake Shange

Introduction

First published in 1975 and praised by *The New Yorker* for "encompassing . . . every feeling a woman has ever had," *for colored girls who have considered suicide/when the rainbow is enuf* uses a complement of female narrators to examine what it is like to be of color and female in America. More than thirty-five years after its inception, the Obie Award–winning *for colored girls* continues to be read and performed around the country and throughout the world.

In her new introduction to the work, Ntozake Shange reflects on the legacy of her best-known work: "*for colored girls* still is a women's trip, and the connection we can make through it, with each other and for each other, is to empower us all."

Discussion Questions

1. How does "dark phrases," the opening poem of *for colored girls*, evoke the psychological states of the many narrators of the work in these lines: "she's half-notes scattered/ without rhythm/ no tune/ sing her sighs/ sing the song of her possibilities. . . ." (page 19)? How might the phrase "sing the song of her possibilities" allude to Walt Whitman's "Song of Myself": "I celebrate myself, and sing myself . . ."? In what ways is *for colored girls* a celebration of the women it profiles?

2. In "graduation nite," the speaker loses her virginity in a Buick the same night as her high school graduation. How does her ecstatic embrace of adulthood in lines like "WE WAZ GROWN   WE WAZ FINALLY GROWN" hint at both her innocence and its loss (page 23)? Of the two rites of passage detailed in this poem, which seems to affect the poem's speaker, the lady in yellow, more profoundly, and why?

3. How does the end of an affair narrated by the lady in red in "no assistance," capture the pathos of a romantic break-up: "this note is attached to a plant/ i've been watering since the day i met you/ you may water it/ yr damn self" (page 28)? How does the disappointed lady in red fit into the spectrum of "colored girls" that Shange profiles in this work?

4. How does the author's juxtaposition of a poem about rape, "latent rapists'" (pages 31–35), with a poem about abortion, "abortion cycle #1" (pages 36–37), highlight the sexual vulnerabilities and dangers faced by many of her female speakers? How does the sequence of poems up to this point in *for colored girls* establish a narrative of sexual awakening, sexual experience, and sexual anguish? To what extent do you think the author intends this series of events to be representative of the experience of women of color more generally?

5. How does the appearance of Sechita in the poem of the same name change the direction of the narrative in *for colored girls* (page 37)? How did this shift have an impact on you as a reader? Is Sechita a sympathetic figure?

6. In the poem "toussaint," the lady in brown describes an incident from childhood where she was disqualified from winning a library contest held for a "colored child" who could "read/ 15 books in three weeks" because she rhapsodized about a book from the adult reading room about Haitian revolutionary Toussaint L'Ouverture (pages 39–44). How does this poem comment on racial inequality both directly and indirectly? How does the narrator's chance encounter with Toussaint Jones enable her to move beyond her obsession with L'Ouverture?

7. In the poem "pyramid," about three girlfriends and the one man they all desire—"we all saw him at the same time/ & he saw us"—how would you characterize the author's depiction of female friendship (pages 53–56)? How does the male romantic interest in "pyramid" compare with the author's other depictions of boys and men in *for colored girls*?

8. How does the sequence of four "no more love poems" (pages 53–63) connect to the visions of romantic love developed in *for colored girls*? Why does each of the speakers of the "no more love poems" reject love, and what do their rejections suggest about the kinds of love they are offered in return?

9. How do the poems "somebody almost walked off wid alla my stuff" (pages 63–65) and "sorry" (pages 66–68) seem to be in dialogue with each other? What do both poems have in common? How does the author's decision to blur the boundaries between poems impact your sense of the progress of the narrative as a whole? Given that *for colored girls* is meant to be performed, how might this blurring of transitions be strategic?

10. How does the relationship between Crystal and Beau Willie, depicted in "a nite with beau willie brown" (pages 78–84) capture the terror of domestic

violence? How does the author's decision to end the poem with Crystal's line, "but I cd only whisper/ & he dropped em," emphasize the powerlessness of the victims of domestic violence?

11. *for colored girls* has elicited criticism from some male readers who feel that they are unfairly stereotyped in the work as abusive or violent by virtue of their gender. Do you agree or disagree with this critique? Why might the author have chosen to explore the darker side of relationships between women and men in this work, and how does her decision affect your understanding of the gender divide in our culture?

12. "positive" is one of the poems that has been added to this edition of *for colored girls*. How does this new poem carry the book into the twenty-first century?

13. Of the many poems in *for colored girls*, which did you find most powerful and why? The title of the collection alludes to colored women who have considered suicide. What part, if any, does suicide seem to play in the scenarios described in the individual poems?

Enhance Your Book Club

1. Stage a dramatic reading of *for colored girls*. Decide as a group how much of the poem will be performed, and assign each member of your book club a role. You might consider inviting friends or family members as an audience. After the presentation, discuss with your group how the emotional impact of the work changes when it is performed.

2. Which of the rites of passage and femininity explored in *for colored girls* did you feel resonated most closely with your own life experiences? Which of the narrators did you feel most closely aligned with and why? Did any of the lines in the work as a whole ring especially true to you? Which ones? You may want to compare experiences with fellow book club members.

3. *for colored girls* is a choreopoem, a work that combines poetry and dance as a unique literary genre. If you were to write a choreopoem about some aspect of your life experiences, what time periods would you focus on? What moments in your life have shaped you most indelibly? Who would you cast in the chorus of back-up voices who would support this rendering of your life? Try writing a choreopoem about a special event in your life and share with your reading group members.

NTOZAKE SHANGE is a renowned playwright, poet, and novelist. Her works include *Some Sing, Some Cry*, which she wrote with Ifa Bayeza; *Betsey Brown*; and *Sassafrass, Cypress & Indigo*. Among her honors and awards are fellowships from the Guggenheim Foundation and the Lila Wallace–Reader's Digest Fund, and a Pushcart Prize. A graduate of Barnard and recipient of a master's in American Studies from the University of Southern California, she lives in Brooklyn.